First World War
and Army of Occupation
War Diary
France, Belgium and Germany

58 DIVISION
Headquarters, Branches and Services
Adjutant and Quarter-Master General
3 September 1915 - 28 February 1916

WO95/2992/1

The Naval & Military Press Ltd
www.nmarchive.com
Published in association with The National Archives

Published by

The Naval & Military Press Ltd

Unit 10 Ridgewood Industrial Park,

Uckfield, East Sussex,

TN22 5QE England

Tel: +44 (0) 1825 749494

www.naval-military-press.com

www.nmarchive.com

This diary has been reprinted in facsimile from the original. Any imperfections are inevitably reproduced and the quality may fall short of modern type and cartographic standards.

© **Crown Copyright**
Images reproduced by permission of The National Archives, London, England, 2015.

Contents

Document type	Place/Title	Date From	Date To
Heading	WO95/2992/1		
Heading	Uk 58 Division (2/1 London Div)		
War Diary		03/09/1915	25/11/1915
War Diary	Ipswich	01/12/1915	28/02/1916

WO 95/2992/1

UK

58 DIVISION
(2/1 LONDON DIV)

AQMG

1915 SEP — 1916 FEB

WAR DIARY
or
INTELLIGENCE SUMMARY

Army Form C. 2118

(Erase heading not required.)

Place	Date	Hour	Summary of Events and Information	Remarks and references to Appendices
	1915.			
Sept.	3rd.		40 other ranks 2/7th Bn London Regt. arrived from London.	
"	4th.		80 do 2/9th do arrived from 3/9th Bn.	
"	5th.		8 officers 2/10th Bn. London Regt. left for overseas.	
			10 do 2/11th do do	
"	17th.		18 other ranks 3/3rd Bn. London Regt. transferred to 100th Prov. Battn.	
"	18th.		49 do do to 3rd Line.	
"	19th		1st London Casualty Clearing Station arrived Ipswich from London.	
"	21st		1 Officer (condg.) 80 other ranks 2/5th Bn London Regt left for overseas.	
"	22nd		1/4th How. Bde R.F.A. left for 36th (Ulster) Division.	
			1/1st Lon. Bde. R.F.A. ditto. 1/3rd Lon. Bde. left for 36th (Ulster) Divn.	
"	23rd		116 remounts arrived from Taunton.	
"	24th		1/2nd London Bde. R.F.A. left for 36th (Ulster) Division.	
"	24th		2/4th How. Bde R.F.A. arrived Ipswich.	
"	25th		2/1st London Hvy Bty R.G.A. arrived Ipswich.	
			2/1st Lon. Bde. R.F.A. arrived Ipswich.	
			2/3rd ditto arrived Framlingham	
"	27th		2/2nd ditto arrived Saxmundham.	

Ipswich.
6/10/15.

[signature]
for Brig. General.
Commanding 58th (London) Divn.

Army Form C. 2118

WAR DIARY or INTELLIGENCE SUMMARY Administrative

(Erase heading not required.)

Instructions regarding War Diaries and Intelligence Summaries are contained in F. S. Regs., Part II. and the Staff Manual respectively. Title Pages will be prepared in manuscript.

[Stamp: 58 LONDON DIVISION GENERAL STAFF 6 - NOV. 1915]

Date	Hour	Summary of Events and Information	Remarks and references to Appendices
1915. October			
2		1 Offr. 71 other ranks from 3/7th Bn. London Regt to 2/7th Bn. London Regt. 2/1st and 2/2nd London Field Coys R.E. left Wickham Market for Needham Market.	
12		2 Offrs 35 other ranks No 2 Coy A.S.C. left Ipswich for Malta.	
19		1 Officer 47 other ranks 2/2nd London Field Coy R.E. left for overseas.	
22		2 Officers 169 other ranks 2/6th Bn London Regt. drafted to 3/6th Bn.	
23		2/2nd London Bde R.F.A. left Saxmundham for Woodbridge.	
26		2/6th Bn London Regt left Ipswich for Stowmarket.	
28		2/9th Bn London Regt left Woodbridge for Ipswich.	
29		31 other ranks A.S.C. arrived Ipswich from London. 69 Remounts arrived from Kettering. 12 do do London.	
30		250 Remounts arrived from Shirehampton. 2 Officers 234 other ranks 2/7th Bn London Regt left Ipswich for 3/7th Battn.	

Ipswich.
5/11/15.

[signature]
Brig.-General.
Commanding 58th (London) Division.

Army Form C. 2118

Instructions regarding War Diaries and Intelligence Summaries are contained in F.S. Regs., Part II. and the Staff Manual respectively. Title Pages will be prepared in manuscript.

WAR DIARY
or
INTELLIGENCE SUMMARY
(Erase heading not required.)

Place	Date	Hour	Summary of Events and Information	Remarks and references to Appendices
	1915.			
	November 1st		2/10th Battn. London Regt. arrived Ipswich from Bromeswell.	
	2nd		100 R. and 60 L.D. horses arrived from Ormskirk.	
	5th		29 R and 92 L.D. Horses arrived from Ormskirk.	
	10th		120 H.D. Horses arrived from Larkhill.	
	12th		34 L.D. Horses arrived from Shirehampton.	
			1/1st London Heavy Battery R.G.A. moved from Warren Heath to Hadleigh.	
			2/1st do do	
	14th		105 R. and 31 H.D. Horses arrived from Beccles.	
	16th		1/5th London Field Coy. R.E. (6 Offrs 211 Other ranks) arrived Claydon from Esher.	
	18th		65th Field Bakery and 56th Field Butchery A.S.C. arrived from Aldershot.	
	20th		Divl Train Bakery Section (12 other ranks) departed for Aldershot.	
	21st		1/1st ❤oy. A.S.C. arrived from Malta.	
	24th		48 H.D. Horses arrived from Northern Command.	
			26 R. and 10 L.D. Horses arrived from Shirehampton.	
	25th		24 R. Horses arrived from Romsey.	

Dec. 5th 1915.

[signature] Brigadier General.
Commanding 58th (London) Division.

Army Form C. 2118

WAR DIARY
or
INTELLIGENCE SUMMARY
(Erase heading not required.)

Instructions regarding War Diaries and Intelligence Summaries are contained in F.S. Regs., Part II. and the Staff Manual respectively. Title Pages will be prepared in manuscript.

Place	Date	Hour	Summary of Events and Information	Remarks and references to Appendices
Ipswich.	1915. Decr. 1st.		Nos 284 to 288 Depot Units of Supply arived in the Division from Aldershot.	
	" 3rd.		35 other Ranks 2/6th Bn London Regt. transferred to 3/6th Battn.	
			No 511 H.T. Coy A.S.C. arrived Ipswich from Lowestoft.	
			17 Other Ranks 2/6th Bn. London Regt. transferred to 101st Prov. Battn.	
	" 4th.		40 Other Ranks 2/6th Bn. London Regt. transferred to 3rd Line.	
			17 do do do to 100th Prov. Battn.	
	" 10th.		63 H.D. Horses arrived from Southern Command.	
	" 16th.		58 do do do from Warminster.	
	" 20th.		7 do do do from Northern Command.	

Ipswich.
5/12/15.

Brig.-General.
Commanding 58th (London) Division.

6 - JAN. 1916
58th (LONDON) DIVISION
GENERAL STAFF

Army Form C. 2118

WAR DIARY
or
INTELLIGENCE SUMMARY

(Erase heading not required.)

Administrative Staff.

Instructions regarding War Diaries and Intelligence Summaries are contained in F.S. Regs., Part II. and the Staff Manual respectively. Title Pages will be prepared in manuscript.

Place	Date	Hour	Summary of Events and Information	Remarks and references to Appendices
	1916. January 3rd		54 Other Ranks 2/12th Bn. London Regt. transferred to 3/12th Battalion.	
	" 4th		57 Other Ranks transferred from 3/12th Bn. London Regt. to 2/12th Battn.	
	" 6th		2/6th Battn. London Regt. moved by road to SUDBURY from STOWMARKET, and accommodated in Billets.	
	" 8th		Brig.Gen. G.P. Hunt, C.M.G. assumed Command of the 173rd Infantry Brigade vice Col. H.C. Cholmondeley C.B.	
	" 13th		Following Units placed under Orders for Overseas:- 2/1st & 2/2nd London Field Coys. R.E., Divisional Signal Coy. R.E., 2/1st, 2/2nd, & 2/3rd London Field Ambulances, Mobile Vety. Section, Divisional Cyclist Company.	
			Brig. Gen. E.J. Granet O.B. assumed Command of Divl. Artillery vice Col. F. Beaver, R.A.	
	" 15th		205 L.D. Horses arrived from Ormskirk.	
	" 17th		Brig.Gen. C. de Winton assumed Command of the 175th Infantry Brigade vice Col. G. Pleydell Bouverie.	
	" 18th		Horses of Units under Orders for Overseas inspected by Major Richardson, D.S.O.	
	" 19th		Divisional Signal Company proceeded to BALDOCK on a Course.	
	" 21st		148 Derby Reservists joined Division for various Units.	
	" 22nd		223 Derby Reservists joined Division for various Units.	
			93 Riding and 10 L.D. Horses arrived from Ormskirk.	
	" 24th		217 Derby Reservists joined Division for various Units.	
			Capt. W. Awde took up duties as A.D.V.S. Division vice Lt.Col. H.M.Maxwell posted to Hdqrs Central Force as A.D.V.S.	
	" 25th		282 Derby Reservists joined Division for various Units.	
	" 26th		186 Derby Reservists joined Division for various Units.	
	" 27th		175 Derby Reservists joined Division for various Units.	
	" 29th		197 Derby Reservists joined Division for various Units.	
			1/1st London Heavy Battery R.G.A. placed under Orders for Overseas.	
	" 31st		166 Derby Reservists joined Division for various Units.	

S.G. Tidu
Colonel,
A.A. & Q.M.G.
58th (London) Divn.

WAR DIARY

INTELLIGENCE SUMMARY

Administrative Army Form C. 2118

(Erase heading not required.)

Instructions regarding War Diaries and Intelligence Summaries are contained in F. S. Regs., Part II. and the Staff Manual respectively. Title Pages will be prepared in manuscript.

Place	Date	Hour	Summary of Events and Information	Remarks and references to Appendices
	1916			
	Feb 1		195 Derby Reservists arrived in the Division.	
	2		148 " " " " " "	
	3		148 " " " " " "	
	4		58 " " " " " "	
	9		162 " " " " " "	
	10		122 " " " " " "	
	11		96 " " " " " "	
			1/1st London Heavy Battery left for Woolwich.	
			Divisional Signal Company left for Overseas.	
	12		134 Derby Reservists arrived in the Division.	
	13		22 " " " " " "	
	14		144 " " " " " "	
	15		55 " " " " " "	
			Major Maitland Makgill Crichton took up duties of G.S.O. II vice Major S. J. Jervis	
	16		10 Derby Reservists arrived in the Division.	
	21		54 " " " " " "	
	21		2/1st, 2/2nd, 2/3rd Field Ambulances, 2/1st and 2/2nd Field Companies, R.E. left the Division for Overseas.	
	22		2/1st, 2/2nd and 2/3rd Home Counties Field Ambulances, Arrived in the Division.	
			Major Miles took up duties of D.A.D.M.S.	
			203 Derby Reservists arrived in the Division.	
	23		75 " " " " " "	
			2/1st and 2/2nd Wessex Field Companies, R.E., and Wessex Divisional Signal Company, R.E., arrived in the Division.	
	24		68 Derby Reservists arrived in the Division.	
			"B" Squadron, 2/2nd County of London Yeomanry arrived in the Division.	
	27		1/5th London Field Company, R.E., left for Brightlingsea on a course.	
	28		Divisional Signal Company left for Baldock on a Course.	
			Remainder of 2/2nd County of London Yeomanry arrived in Division.	
			37 Derby Reservists arrived in the Division.	
			152 Light Draught Mules arrived.	

G. K. Steel
Colonel,
A. A. & Q. M. G.
58th (LONDON) DIVISION.

www.ingramcontent.com/pod-product-compliance
Lightning Source LLC
Chambersburg PA
CBHW081515160426
43193CB00014B/2695